Practical Pre-School Books

Planning
for Learning
through
Weather

by Rachel Sparks Linfield Illustrated by Cathy Hughes

Contents

Published by Step Forward Publishing Limited

St Jude's Church, Dulwich Road, Herne Hill, London, SE24 0PB Tel. 020 7738 5454

Revised edition © Step Forward Publishing Limited 2008

First edition © Step Forward Publishing Limited 2005

www.practicalpreschoolbooks.com

Planning for Learning through Weather ISBN: 978 1 90457 556 6

Making plans

Why plan?

The purpose of planning is to make sure that all children enjoy a broad and balanced curriculum. All planning should be useful. Plans are working documents that you spend time preparing, but which should later repay your efforts. Try to be concise. This will help you in finding information quickly when you need it.

Long-term plans

Preparing a long-term plan, which maps out the curriculum during a year or even two, will help you to ensure that you are providing a variety of activities and are meeting the statutory requirements of the *Statutory Framework for the Early Years Foundation Stage* (2007).

Your long-term plan need not be detailed. Divide the time period over which you are planning into fairly equal sections, such as half terms. Choose a topic for each section. Young children benefit from making links between the new ideas they encounter so as you select each topic, think about the time of year in which you plan to do it. A topic about minibeasts will not be very successful in November!

Although each topic will address all the learning areas, some could focus on a specific area. For example, a topic on 'Weather' would lend itself well to activities relating to Creative Development and Knowledge and Understanding of the World. Another topic might particularly encourage

the appreciation of stories. Try to make sure that you provide a variety of topics in your long-term plans such as:

Autumn 1	Nursery rhymes
Autumn 2	Autumn/Christmas
Spring 1	Weather
Spring 2	Shopping
Summer 1	What are things made of?
Summer 2	Minibeasts

Medium-term plans

Medium-term plans will outline the contents of a topic in a little more detail. One way to start this process is by brainstorming on a large piece of paper. Work with your team writing down all the activities you can think of which are relevant to the topic. As you do this it may become clear that some activities go well together. Think about dividing them into themes. The topic of 'Weather', for example, has weekly themes such as 'Sunny days', 'Rain and clouds', 'Stormy days', 'Ice, frost and snow', 'Measuring and forecasting the weather' and 'Using the weather'. At this stage it is helpful to make a chart. Write the theme ideas down the side of the chart and put a different area of learning at the top of each column. Now you can insert your brainstormed ideas and quickly see where there are gaps. As you complete the chart take account of children's earlier experiences and provide opportunities for them to progress.

Refer back to the *Statutory Framework for the Early Years Foundation Stage* and check that you have addressed as many different aspects of it as you can. Once all your medium-term plans are complete make sure that there are no neglected areas.

Day-to-day plans

The plans you make for each day will outline aspects such as:

● resources needed;
● the way in which you might introduce activities;
● safety;
● the organisation of adult help;
● size of the group;

Making plans

- timing;
- key vocabulary;
- individual needs.

Identify the learning and ELGs that each activity is intended to promote. Make a note of any assessments or observations that you are likely to carry out. After using the plans, make notes of activities that were particularly successful, or any changes you would make another time.

A final note

Planning should be seen as flexible. Not all groups meet every day, and not all children attend every day. Any part of the plan can be used independently, stretched over a longer period or condensed to meet the needs of any group. You will almost certainly adapt the activities as children respond to them in different ways and bring their own ideas, interests and enthusiasms. The important thing is to ensure that children are provided with a varied and enjoyable curriculum that meets their individual developing needs.

Using the book

- Collect or prepare suggested resources as listed on page 21.
- Read the section which outlines links to the Early Learning Goals (pages 4-7) and explains the rationale for the topic of 'Weather'.
- For each weekly theme two activities are described in detail as an example to help you in your planning and preparation. Key vocabulary, questions and learning opportunities are identified.
- The skills chart on page 23 will help you to see at a glance which aspects of children's development are being addressed as a focus each week.
- As children take part in the 'Weather' topic activities, their learning will progress. 'Collecting evidence' on page 22 explains how you might monitor children's achievements.
- Find out on page 20 how the topic can be brought together in a grand finale involving parents, children and friends.
- There is additional material to support the working

partnership of families and children in the form of a 'Home links' page, and a photocopiable 'Parent's page' at the back of the book.

It is important to appreciate that the ideas presented in this book will only be a part of your planning. Many activities that will be taking place as routine in your group may not be mentioned. For example, it is assumed that sand, dough, water, puzzles, floor toys and large scale apparatus are part of the ongoing pre-school experience, as are the opportunities to develop ICT skills. Role-play areas, stories, rhymes and singing, and group discussion times are similarly assumed to be happening each week, although they may not be a focus for described activities. Groups should also ensure that there is a balance of adult-led and child-initiated activities.

This book on weather could be used for a complete topic. Alternatively a week's activities could be used throughout the year at appropriate times. The 'Ice, frost and snow' week, in particular, is exciting when children can have a direct, hands-on experience of snow.

Using this book in Northern Ireland, Scotland and Wales

Although the curriculum guidelines in Northern Ireland, Scotland and Wales differ, the activities in this book are still appropriate for use throughout the United Kingdom. They are designed to promote the development of early skills and to represent good practice in the early years

Glossary

EYFS: Early Years Foundation Stage
ELG: Early Learning Goal

Using the 'Early Learning Goals'

Having chosen your topic and made your medium-term plans you can use the *Statutory Framework for the Early Years Foundation Stage* to highlight the key learning opportunities your activities will address. The Early Learning Goals are split into six areas: Personal, Social and Emotional Development; Communication, Language and Literacy; Problem Solving, Reasoning and Numeracy; Knowledge and Understanding of the World; Physical Development and Creative Development. Do not expect each of your topics to cover every goal but your long-term plans should allow for all of them to be addressed by the time a child enters Year 1.

The following section lists the Early Learning Goals in point form to show what children are expected to be able to do in each area of learning by the time they enter Year 1. These points will be used throughout this book to show how activities for a topic on 'Weather' link to these expectations. For example, Personal, Social and Emotional Development point 7 is 'form good relationships with adults and peers'. Activities suggested which provide the opportunity for children to do this will have the reference PS7. This will enable you to see which Early Learning Goals are covered in a given week and plan for areas to be revisited and developed.

In addition, you can make sure that activities offer variety in the goals to be encountered. Often a similar activity may be carried out to achieve different Early Learning Goals. For example, during this topic children use shapes to print circles on suns. Children will be developing areas of Problem Solving, Reasoning and Numeracy as they recognise shapes and talk about their properties. Also, they will be using creative skills as they choose colours and shapes to form the patterns. It is important, therefore, that activities have clearly defined goals so that these may be emphasised during the activity and for recording purposes.

Personal, Social and Emotional Development (PS)

This area of learning covers important aspects of development that affect the way children learn, behave and relate to others.

By the end of the EYFS, children should:

PS1 Continue to be interested, excited and motivated to learn.

PS2 Be confident to try new activities, initiate ideas and speak in a familiar group.

PS3 Maintain attention, concentrate and sit quietly when appropriate.

PS4 Have a developing awareness of their own needs, views and feelings and be sensitive to the needs, views and feelings of others.

PS5 Have a developing respect for their own cultures and beliefs and those of other people.

PS6 Respond to significant experiences, showing a range of feelings, when appropriate.

PS7 Form good relationships with adults and peers.

PS8 Work as part of a group or class, taking turns and sharing fairly, understanding that there needs to be agreed values and codes of behaviour for groups of people, including adults and children, to work together harmoniously.

PS9 Understand what is right, what is wrong, and why.

PS10 Consider the consequences of their words and actions for themselves and others.

PS11 Dress and undress independently and manage their own personal hygiene.

PS12 Select and use activities and resources independently.

PS13 Understand that people have different needs, views, cultures and beliefs, that need to be treated with respect.

PS14 Understand that they can expect others to treat their needs, views, cultures and beliefs with respect.

The topic of 'Weather' offers many opportunities for children's personal, social and emotional development. Time spent discussing what the children like to do and wear in different weather will encourage them to speak in a group, to be interested and to consider consequences. By speaking about people who have been affected by extreme weather conditions the children will respond to significant experiences, showing a range of feelings when appropriate. Many of the areas outlined above, though, will be covered on an almost incidental basis as children carry out the activities described in this book for the other areas of learning. During undirected free choice times they will be developing PS12 while any small group activity that involves working with an adult will help children to work towards PS7.

Communication, Language and Literacy (L)

By the end of the EYFS, children should:

L1 Interact with others, negotiating plans and activities and taking turns in conversation.

L2 Enjoy listening to and using spoken and written language, and readily turn to it in their play and learning.

L3 Sustain attentive listening, responding to what they have heard by relevant comments, questions or actions.

L4 Listen with enjoyment and respond to stories, songs and other music, rhymes and poems and make up their own stories, songs, rhymes and poems.

L5 Extend their vocabulary, exploring the meaning and sounds of new words.

L6 Speak clearly and audibly with confidence and control and show awareness of the listener.

L7 Use language to imagine and recreate roles and experiences.

L8 Use talk to organise, sequence and clarify thinking, ideas, feelings and events.

L9 Hear and say sounds in words in the order in which they occur.

L10 Link sounds to letters, naming and sounding the letters of the alphabet.

L11 Use their phonic knowledge to write simple regular words and make phonetically plausible attempts at more complex words.

L12 Explore and experiment with sounds, words and texts.

L13 Retell narratives in the correct sequence, drawing on language patterns of stories.

L14 Read a range of familiar and common words and simple sentences independently.

L15 Know that print carries meaning, and in English, is read from left to right and top to bottom.

L16 Show an understanding of the elements of stories such as main character, sequence of events and openings, and how information can be found in non-fiction texts to answer questions about where, who, why and how.

L17 Attempt writing for different purposes, using features of different forms such as lists, stories and instructions.

L18 Write their own names and other things such as labels and captions and begin to form sentences, sometimes using punctuation.

L19 Use a pencil and hold it effectively to form recognisable letters, most of which are correctly formed.

A number of the activities suggested for the theme of the 'Weather' are based on well known picture books and stories. They allow children to enjoy sharing the books and to respond in a variety of ways to what they hear, reinforcing and extending their vocabulary. Throughout the topic opportunities are described in which children are encouraged to use descriptive vocabulary and to see some of their ideas recorded in both pictures and words as they collaborate to write weather poems, labels for a weather map and make a big book.

The theme of 'Weather' provides a meaningful context for Problem Solving, Reasoning and Numeracy activities. Children are given opportunities to explore shapes and size as they weigh snowballs made from white socks filled with lentils and print with circular objects on to paper suns. They can count when they play dice games such as a snowman 'beetle drive' and use the snowman counting rhyme. The Beaufort Scale for wind force allows children to recognise written numbers. The 'Weather day' is a wonderful opportunity for the children to gain awareness of coins, to buy, sell, sort and count.

Knowledge and Understanding of the World (K)

By the end of the EYFS, children should:

K1   Investigate objects and materials by using all of their senses as appropriate.
K2   Find out about, and identify, some features of living things, objects and events they observe.
K3   Look closely at similarities, differences, patterns and change.
K4   Ask questions about why things happen and how things work.
K5   Build and construct with a wide range of objects, selecting appropriate resources and adapting their work where necessary.
K6   Select the tools and techniques they need to shape, assemble and join materials they are using.
K7   Find out about and identify the uses of everyday technology and use information and communication technology and programmable toys to support their learning.
K8   Find out about past and present events in their own lives, and those of their families and other people they know.
K9   Observe, find out about and identify features in the place they live and the natural world.
K10 Find out about their environment, and talk about those features they like and dislike.
K11 Begin to know about their own cultures and beliefs and those of other people.

The topic of 'Weather' offers many opportunities for children to make observations, to ask questions and to compare. As they observe icing sugar frost patterns, a melting iceberg and shadows, and make rain encourage them to notice details. There are many opportunities for going outside. Through all the activities encourage children to talk and to give reasons for choices and observations.

Problem Solving, Reasoning and Numeracy (N)

By the end of the EYFS, children should:

N1   Say and use number names in order in familiar contexts .
N2   Count reliably up to ten everyday objects.
N3   Recognise numerals 1 to 9.
N4   Use developing mathematical ideas and methods to solve practical problems.
N5   In practical activities and discussion, begin to use the vocabulary involved in adding and subtracting.
N6   Use language such as 'more' or 'less' to compare two numbers.
N7   Find one more or one less than a number from one to ten.
N8   Begin to relate addition to combining two groups of objects and subtraction to 'taking away'.
N9   Use language such as 'greater', 'smaller', 'heavier' or 'lighter' to compare quantities.
N10 Talk about, recognise and recreate simple patterns.
N11 Use language such as 'circle' or 'bigger' to describe the shape and size of solids and flat shapes
N12 Use everyday words to describe position.

Physical Development (PD)

By the end of the EYFS, children should:

PD1   Move with confidence, imagination and in safety.

PD2   Move with control and coordination.

PD3   Travel around, under, over and through balancing and climbing equipment.

PD4   Show awareness of space, of themselves and of others.

PD5   Recognise the importance of keeping healthy and those things which contribute to this.

PD6   Recognise the changes that happen to their bodies when they are active.

PD7   Use a range of small and large equipment.

PD8   Handle tools, objects, construction and malleable materials safely and with increasing control.

Activities such as using snowy dough and blowing and chasing bubbles will offer experience of PD8. Through pretending to dress for a variety of weather conditions and doing a kite 'follow my leader', they will have the opportunity to move with control and imagination. While using a range of small equipment such as balls and jumping in imaginary hoop puddles children will be developing coordination and control.

Creative Development (C)

By the end of the EYFS, children should:

C1   Respond in a variety of ways to what they see, hear, smell, touch and feel.

C2   Express and communicate their ideas, thoughts and feelings by using a widening range of materials, suitable tools, imaginative and role-play, movement, designing and making, and a variety of songs and musical instruments.

C3   Explore colour, texture, shape, form and space in two or three dimensions.

C4   Recognise and explore how sounds can be changed, sing simple songs from memory, recognise repeated sounds and sound patterns and match movements to music.

C5   Use their imagination in art and design, music, dance, imaginative and role-play and stories.

During this topic children will experience working with a variety of materials as they make collages with pictures from mail order catalogues, travel brochures and magazines; do wax resist paintings and make snowy scenes in shoe boxes. They will be able to develop their imaginations and skills of painting and colour mixing as they paint self-portraits. Throughout all the activities encourage children to talk about what they see and feel as they communicate their ideas in painting, collage work, music and role play.

Week 1
Sunny days

Personal, Social and Emotional Development

- Introduce the topic of weather by showing the group a collection of clothes. Talk about which clothes would be appropriate for different weather. Play the weather game (see activity opposite). (PS2, 8)
- Read 'Seaside' from *Out and About through the year* by Shirley Hughes. Talk about the kinds of things that children enjoy doing on sunny days. Has anyone been to the seaside? (PS5)
- Look at pictures of sunny days in books, on postcards and in travel brochures. Talk about the precautions people should take when they go out in the sun (wear sun hats and sun cream, drink water). Make posters to remind people to wear sun hats. (PS9)

Communication, Language and Literacy

- Make a collection of words that rhyme with sun. Use the words to make a sunny poem. (It could be a nonsense rhyme!) (L4, 10, 12)
- Give each child a sun cut from orange paper. Ask them to draw what they enjoy doing most on a sunny day. Scribe sentences to explain the pictures and stick the suns into a large, group book. (L3, 8)
- Enjoy sharing *Winnie at the Seaside* by Korley Paul and Valerie Thomas, *Splash* by Jane Hissey or another tale about a trip to the seaside. Encourage children to realise why people prefer it to be sunny when they're at the seaside. (L3, 4)

Problem Solving, Reasoning and Numeracy

- Work with a small group. Give each child a circle of orange card surrounded by ten lolly sticks as rays. Ask children, in turn, to roll a die with digits one to three and to remove the corresponding number of rays. After each turn, count how many rays remain. The game finishes when a sun has lost all its rays. (N1, 2, 3)
- Repeat the sun game but this time begin with the sun and add the rays. After five turns, see who has the most rays. (N1, 2, 3)
- Look at pictures of sunsets that include circular suns. Talk about the shape of the suns. Look through magazines for objects that are circular. Encourage children to use the word 'circle' and to notice their size. (N11)

Knowledge and Understanding of the World

- On a sunny day encourage children to investigate how shadows are made. **Remind children never to look directly at the sun.** (K2, 3, 4)
- Make sunlight catchers. Give each child a circle of white card about 15cm in diameter. Provide shiny paper, metallic ribbons, glitter glue and sheets of cellophane/acetate to stick on to the circles. When dry, hang the catchers in a sunny window. Encourage children to describe the colours reflected in the sun. (K3)
- Place a flowering plant on a sunny windowsill so that you can see how plants grow towards the light. If appropriate, plant seeds or bulbs to show the importance of sun for growth. (K3)

Physical Development

- Enjoy using outdoor equipment on a sunny day. Remind the children of the importance of sun protection, such as sun hats. Afterwards talk about the changes that happen to our bodies when we are active. (PD5, 6)
- Enjoy using outdoor sand trays. Encourage children to build sandcastles and to imagine that they are at the seaside. (PD8)

Creative Development

- Use paper bowls to make sun bonnets (see activity opposite). (C3)
- Provide large paper circles and red and yellow paints. Show children how to mix a variety of oranges. Enjoy covering the circles in orange dots. (C3)
- Make shadow puppets by cutting animals and people from greetings cards and attaching them with tape to lolly sticks. Use them outside on a sunny day to make up stories and to retell familiar ones. (C5)

Activity: The weather game

Learning opportunity: Collaborating to decide which clothes to wear for different weather.

Early Learning Goal: Personal, Social and Emotional Development. Children should be confident to try activities, initiate ideas and speak in a familiar group. They should work as part of a group or class, taking turns and sharing fairly, understanding that there needs to be agreed values and codes of behaviour for groups of people, including adults and children, to work together harmoniously.

Resources: Collection of clothes and accessories for different weathers for children to dress up in (for example sun glasses, Wellington boots, safe umbrella, large swimming trunks, woollen mittens, rain coat); cards with a picture and word for each weather (sun, rain, snow, wind, fog); picture books showing people dressed for different weathers.

Organisation: Whole group sitting on the floor.

Key vocabulary: Sun, rain, snow, wind, fog, weather, cold, hot, dry, wet, names for the clothing and accessories.

What to do: Remind children about routines for taking turns and listening such as looking at the person who is speaking. Look through a selection of picture books that depict people dressed for different weathers. Focus on the clothes, and talk about why they are or are not appropriate for the weather. What do the children like to wear when it is sunny?

Show the group the weather cards. Ask children to say the weather each card shows. Invite a child to select a card and to put on two things that would be good to wear in that weather. As a group, decide whether the chosen clothes/accessories are sensible. Repeat this with the rest of the group so that everyone is dressed in clothes for different weather.

To the tune of 'Jingle bells' sing:

> Jingle bells, jingle bells,
> Jingle all the way,
> Oh what fun it is to clap,
> On a sunny, sunny day.

On 'sunny, sunny', any child dressed for the sun should stand up and clap. Repeat the verse for other weathers and with a range of actions such as smile and jump.

Activity: Sun bonnets

Learning opportunity: Decorating paper plates to make sun bonnets.

Early Learning Goal: Creative Development. Children should explore colour, texture, shape, form and space in two or three dimensions.

Resources: Paper bowls (to fit a child's head); felt pens, glue, tissue paper, ribbon or thick wool; hole punch.

Organisation: Small group.

Key vocabulary: Sunny, sunbonnet, names for colours and materials used; protection, protect.

What to do: Ask children why it is important to wear hats in the sun. Talk about the need to protect the back of the neck.

Give each child a paper bowl. Ask them to use the felt pens and scrunched up tissue paper to decorate their sun bonnet. When complete, punch a hole at each side and attach ribbons or wool that can be tied securely under children's chins.

Display

Cover a board with sky blue wallpaper and add an orange border around the edge. Use this as the background for painted suns and your sunny poem. In a nearby window hang the sunlight catchers. On a table put out storybooks that show sunny days, the group's big book and some large dolls or teddies wearing a selection of the sun bonnets you have made, reminding people to wear hats in the sun.

Week 2
Rain and clouds

Personal, Social and Emotional Development

- Talk about the importance of rain for providing water. As a group, make a list of the ways that we use water. Explain why it is important not to waste water. (PS2, 3, 9)
- Look at pictures of countries that have suffered from droughts and also areas where there have been floods. Encourage children to notice the differences. (PS4)
- Enjoy standing outside on a rainy day, dressed in appropriate clothing. Encourage children to notice how the rain falls and feels. Back inside, scribe the children's desriptions of the rain and ask them to paint pictures of rainy days. (PS4, 11)

Communication, Language and Literacy

- Make a collection of poems about the rain such as the traditional 'Doctor Foster went to Gloucester' and 'I hear thunder'; 'Wet' from *Out and About through the year* by Shirley Hughes and 'Clouds' from *Twinkle, Twinkle Chocolate Bar* compiled by John Foster. Enjoy sharing the poems and using percussion instruments to add rainy sound effects. (L4, 12)
- As a group make a list of new creatures to replace 'Incy, Wincy Spider' in the traditional nursery rhyme and words to describe how each one gets up the spout (See activity opposite.). (L4)
- Ask the children to suggest a word to describe rain. Help them to write the words on raindrops cut from card. (L11, 18, 19)

Problem Solving, Reasoning and Numeracy

- Make a collection of Wellington boots. Sort the boots into pairs. Ask the children to count the total number of boots and also the number of pairs. (N1, 2)
- Use hoops to sort the boots into sets according to different criteria such as colour, size, left or right foot and height. After sorting invite the children to find a number card to show how many boots are in each set. (N1, 2, 3)

Knowledge and Understanding of the World

- Investigate what is the best filling for making a rain shaker (see activity opposite). (K1, 10)
- Investigate the best way to 'make rain' in the water tray. Compare sieves, watering cans and plastic containers with holes punched in a variety of sizes. (K3)
- Enjoy sharing the story of Noah's Ark. Make models of the animals that went into the ark. (K6, 11)
- Use a digital camera to take photos of clouds over a week. Compare the shapes, sizes and colours of the clouds. (K3, 7)

Physical Development

- Outside use large brushes to paint with water. Encourage the children to notice how long it takes for the water to evaporate. (PD7)
- Use hoops as imaginary puddles as the children mime the story of getting up, putting on waterproof clothes and boots, putting up an umbrella and enjoying a walk splashing through puddles. (PD1, 2, 4)
- Use playground chalk to sketch large clouds outside. Encourage the children to hop, jump and balance around the edges of the clouds. (PD2)

Creative Development

- Paint pictures on easels with watery paints. Talk about how the paint behaves. (C3)
- As a group make a collage of a rainy sky. Make a collection of rain coloured papers. Tear clouds from the papers and glue them on to grey paper. (C3)

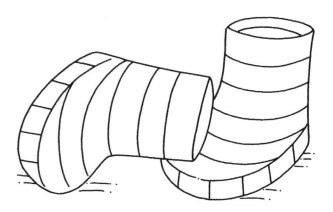

Activity: Who climbed the waterspout?

Learning opportunity: Making up rhymes.

Early learning goal: Communication Language and Literacy. Children should listen with enjoyment... to ...rhymes and make up their own... rhymes and poems.

Resources: Cardboard tubes, scrap pieces of card, sticky Velcro pads, felt pens, scissors, pictures of animals including one of a hippo.

Key vocabulary: Waterspout, spider, raindrops, sunshine.
Organisation: Whole group.

What to do: As a group, enjoy reciting 'Incy wincy spider' with actions. Talk about the vocabulary. What is a waterspout? Why might the spider have climbed up? What did the sun do? Together, look through the pictures of animals. Show one of a hippo. Ask the children to think how it might climb up the spout. Would it crawl, jump, run, stomp? Recite the 'Incy wincy' rhyme with the line 'Shiny, grey hippo stomped up the water spout'. Invite suggestions for other animals and how they climb the spout.

Give each child a piece of card on which to draw an animal. When finished attach a piece of Velcro to its back and also two pieces at the top and bottom of a tube. Scribe the children's lines and use the tubes and animals when reading the whole group's poem.

Activity: Shaking rain

Learning opportunity: Comparing fillings for rain shakers.

Early learning goal: Knowledge and Understanding of the World. Children should investigate objects and materials by using all of their senses as appropriate. They will find out about their environment and talk about those features they like and dislike.

Resources: Small plastic bottles and tubs with lids; range of fillings e.g. rice, lentils, match sticks; stickers; masking tape.

Key vocabulary: Rain, rain shaker, words to describe the rain; quiet, loud, slow, fast, heavy.

Organisation: Whole group introduction, small groups to make the shakers.

What to do: Talk about the way the rain falls at a variety of speeds and sometimes sounds loud, other times quiet. Place a few pieces of rice in a tub. Invite a child to shake as if the rain was falling heavily. Does it sound like heavy rain? What would happen if more rice is put in the tub? Ask a child to try. Explain that today the children are going to make rain shakers to use when they sing songs that have rain in them.

Invite small groups to select the materials they want for their shaker. Once they are content that it makes their desired sound, tape the lid on tightly. Provide stickers to decorate the shakers.

When all the children have made their shakers use them whilst singing a song that mentions the rain such as 'Incy wincy spider' or 'I hear thunder'.\

Display

Cover a board with the rainy sky collages and use it as a background for the decorated boots and umbrellas and the waterspouts and verses. Close by hang up the rain drop words at varying heights. Cover a table with blue or grey cloth and display the rain shakers. Invite the children to write their own name labels for the shakers.

Cover a second board with grey paper. Mount the pictures of countries that have suffered from droughts, and areas where there have been floods, on black paper. Put up the pictures and ask the children to bring in others from their carers' newspapers. In following weeks add pictures of other weathers such as hurricanes and tornados in readiness for the 'Weather Day'.

Week 3
Stormy days

Personal, Social and Emotional Development
- Listen to a piece of classical music that conjures up pictures of a storm. (e.g. 'Spring' from *The Four Seasons* by Vivaldi). Encourage the children to take it in turn to explain how the music makes them feel. (PS4, 8)
- Look at pictures in newspapers of areas that have suffered in storms. Make 'I'm sorry' cards for the people whose lives have been affected. (PS4)

Communication, Language and Literacy
- Write name labels for the stormy and Beaufort Scale paintings (see Knowledge and Understanding of the World and Creative Development). (L18)
- Read *After the Storm* by Nick Butterworth or *Elmer and the Wind* by David McKee. (L4)

Problem Solving, Reasoning and Numeracy
- Match number labels to the paintings of the Beaufort Scale (see Knowledge and Understanding of the World). (N1, 3)
- Make flags with repeating patterns by printing with regular shapes on pieces cut from old white sheets or by sticking paper shapes on A4 sized paper. When completed glue about 2cm of the flag around a 30cm piece of dowel. (N10)
- Give each child an A4 piece of card cut into a kite shape to decorate, and a strip of border role or ribbon to use for a tail. When finished involve the children in displaying the kites in order for their tail lengths. Encourage the children to use positional vocabulary as they place their kites on the board. (N9, 12)

Knowledge and Understanding of the World
- Explain that wind is moving air. Encourage the children to realise that although wind cannot be seen we can see what the wind does. Take the children outside or look through windows to see what the wind can move. (K3, 4, 9)
- On a windy day go for a safe walk outside around the area where the group meets. Take streamers made from pieces of ribbon. Investigate which are the windiest places. Repeat this on another occasion to see whether the places are always windy. (K2, 3, 9)

- Paint pictures to illustrate the Beaufort Scale (see activity opposite). (K3)

Physical Development
- On a windy day enjoy blowing and chasing bubbles. (PD8)
- Tell a story about a stormy day. Encourage the children to mime getting dressed in warm clothes and boots and walking in strong wind that pushes and blows. Make lines with chalk or masking tape for the children to balance along as the wind blows. (PD1, 2)
- Play the traditional flapping fish game. Cut fish from newspaper. Use large pieces of card or magazines to fan and blow the fish into a hoop. When the children have mastered 'being the wind' repeat this activity as a race. (PD7)

Creative Development
- Compose a stormy piece of music (see activity opposite). (C4)

- Provide blue, black and white paint for the painting of stormy pictures on grey paper. Encourage the children to think about how the wind blows and to show movement within their paintings. (C3, 5)
- Use bright coloured finger paints and black card to make swirling, stormy patterns. (C3, 5)

Activity: Painting the Beaufort Scale

Learning opportunity: Painting pictures to show the Beaufort scale and comparing the pictures' details.

Early Learning Goal: Knowledge and Understanding of the World. Children should look closely at similarities, differences…and change.

Resources: A3 sized white or grey paper; paints, brushes.

Key vocabulary: Words mentioned in the Beaufort scale, washing line and pegs with numbers 0-12.

Organisation: Whole group introduction, small groups for the painting

What to do: Remind the children that wind is moving air. Ask them to look through a window. Is it windy today? How do they know? Explain that the Beaufort scale shows how windy it is. Describe how on a day when there is no wind the smoke from a chimney rises straight up and that this is Force 0. Invite a child to peg a zero on the line. Explain other wind forces from the scale and peg up their strength numbers. Tell the group that over the week each child will be able to paint a picture to illustrate one of the force numbers.

Force 0:	Smoke rises vertically.
Force 1:	Smoke drifts.
Force 2:	Leaves rustle.
Force 3:	Small flags flap.
Force 4:	Small branches move. Loose paper is raised.
Force 5:	Small trees start to sway.
Force 6:	It is hard to use an umbrella.
Force 8:	Twigs break from trees.
Force 7:	Whole trees move. It is hard to walk in the wind
Force 9:	Houses are damaged slightly. Roof tiles may be blown off.
Force 10:	Trees are blown down.
Force 11:	At sea waves are high enough to hide ships.
Force 12:	Cars are overturned and buildings are badly damaged. The wind is now a hurricane.

Activity: Stormy Music

Learning opportunity: Collaborating to make a piece of stormy music.

Early Learning Goal: Creative Development. Children should recognise and explore how sounds can be changed…

Resources: Range of percussion instruments; cassette recorder, picture of a storm

Key vocabulary: Stormy, thunder, lightning, loud, quiet, quick, slow.

Organisation: Group of up to ten children sitting on the floor in a circle; picture of a storm.

What to do: Sit in a circle with the percussion instruments in the centre. Show the group the picture of the storm. Talk about the wind, rain, lightning and thunder. Has anyone heard thunder? How does rain sound when it is falling quickly?

Ask each child to select an instrument, and to place it in front of them on the floor. Praise those who do this sensibly. Invite each child, in turn, to play the instrument. Does it sound like the wind/rain/thunder? Can the sound be made louder/quieter/quicker? Say that when you point to someone they must play their instrument to make a steady, tapping noise like rain and that they must keep doing it until you point again. Point at the children in turn until all are tapping, then point one by one until all is quiet. Say that the music was like a stormy night when the rain becomes heavier and heavier and then gradually stops. To make it more like a storm though windy sounds and, perhaps, thunder are needed. Ask for suggestions of ways to make wind and thunder sounds (e.g. flapping stiff card, blowing, a drum). Repeat the stormy music with the added sound effects. When everyone thinks the music cannot be improved, rcord the piece.

Display

Put up the Beaufort pictures in order in lines to show the wind force increasing. Label each one from force 0 to force 12. (When the pictures eventually come down, make them into a big, non-fiction book.) Mount the finger paintings on brightly coloured papers and display them on a board covered with black paper. Ask the children for words to describe their patterns (e.g. swish, swirl, whoosh) and place these between the finger paintings. Place the flags in threes in large, plastic bottles, partly filled with sand on a nearby table.

Week 4
Ice, frost and snow

Personal, Social and Emotional Development

- Talk about appropriate footwear for icy weather. Look through a collection of shoes, trainers, sandals and boots. Examine the soles and select ones to wear in the snow. Encourage the children to say why they would be good. Take rubbings of their soles with thick wax crayons and newsprint paper. (PS2, 5, 9)
- On a frosty day enjoy looking at ice crystals outside. Look for spiders' webs that sparkle with frost. Back inside use glitter paint to record the sparkling webs. (PS4)

Communication, Language and Literacy

- Enjoy sharing *Jolly Snow* by Jane Hissey. Make a list of the ways that the toys made snow. Ask for suggestions of other things that the toys might have tried. (L1, 3, 4)
- Give each child a circle or hexagon cut from white card. As a group, make a list of words to describe snow, ice and frost. Give each child a circle or hexagon cut from white card. Help each child to write one descriptive word on a snowball or snowflake and use these to make an icy mobile. (L11, 18, 19)
- Use pictures cut from travel brochures, magazines and mail order catalogues to make posters of what to wear in snowy and icy weather. (L18)
- Make lists of words that rhyme with ice, frost and snow. Use the words to make a group nonsense rhyme. (L5, 9)

Problem Solving, Reasoning and Numeracy

- Make snowflakes by cutting pieces from white paper circles folded into six sections. Explain that real snowflakes have six 'sections' and that all snowflakes are different. Compare the snowflakes' sizes and shapes. Encourage the children to count the sections and to use the word 'circle'. (N11)
- Play a 'beetle drive' type game based on a snowman. 1 = head, 2 = body, 3 = eyes, 4 = mouth, 5 = nose, 6 = hat. (N1, 2, 3)
- Compare the weights of snowballs made from white socks and lentils (see activity opposite). (N9)

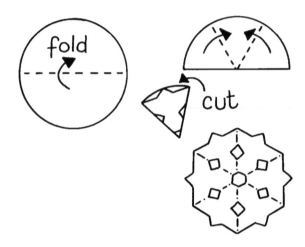

Knowledge and Understanding of the World

- Observe frost patterns in icing sugar (see activity opposite). (K3, 9)
- Ask the children to retell the story of *Jolly Snow* by Jane Hissey from the pictures. Make snow storms from small see through plastic bottles of water. Investigate whether adding sugar, salt, soap powder, desiccated coconut or glitter makes the most realistic snow. Use clear tape to stick a snowy landscape from a winter holiday brochure to the back of the bottle. (K3, 4)
- Make an iceberg by freezing an ice cream container of water. Float the ice in a water tray. Encourage the children to observe how the ice floats and melts. Ensure that the children do not touch the 'iceberg' with their bare hands. (K3, 4)

Taped on lid

Plastic bottle filled with water

Glitter for snow

Physical Development

- Enjoy playing with large and small balls. Encourage the children to imagine they are playing in the snow as they roll and throw 'snowballs'. (PD1, 7)
- Use white modeling dough to make snowy scenes. Provide fir cones to be used as trees. (PD8)

Creative Development

- Provide white card hexagons for the children to decorate with glitter and shiny materials. As a group, arrange the hexagons to make a frosty patchwork. (C2, 3)
- Paint self-portraits of children in outfits for playing in the snow. (C3, 5)
- Provide black paper and white paint and chalk to make night-time snowy scenes. (C3)

Activity: Balancing lentil snowballs

Learning opportunity: Using balancing scales.

Early Learning Goal: Problem Solving, Reasoning and Numeracy. Children should use language such as 'greater', 'smaller', 'heavier' or 'lighter' to compare quantities.

Resources: 2 pan balances; snowballs of varying weights made by putting lentils in the feet end of unwanted, white socks, knotting the ankles and cutting off extra material; small boot, sticky dots, strips of fabric..

Key vocabulary: Heavier, lighter, heaviest, lightest, balance.

Organisation: Small group.

What to do: Show the group the balance. Put the boot in one pan. Ask whether the children can think of anything in the room that would fit in the other pan and be heavier than the boot. Try out some of the suggestions. Can anyone find anything lighter than the boot? The same weight as the boot? During this introduction ensure that the group understand the key words.

Show the group the snowballs. Ask whether they could find two that would make the pans balance. Which is the heaviest/lightest snowball? Can the group arrange the snowballs in order from heaviest to lightest?

Finish by allowing the children to play with the balls to make snowmen by balancing one on top of another. Provide sticky dots for facial features and scraps of fabrics for scarves.

Activity: Sugary frost

Learning opportunity: Observing and describing the formation of frost patterns.

Early Learning Goal: Knowledge and Understanding of the World. Children should look closely at similarities, differences, patterns and change. They will observe, find out about and identify features in the place they live and the natural world.

Resources: Icing sugar, teaspoon, bowl, water, card, thick paint/paste brush, matchsticks, food colourings. (Note: Food colouring stains. Ensure work surfaces are well covered and that children wear overalls. It is best to pour a little colouring into a bowl as the small bottles are easily spilt.)

Key vocabulary: Names for the food colourings' colours; frost, pattern.

Organisation: Small group.

What to do: Mix about 8 heaped teaspoons of icing sugar with 2 teaspoons of water to make a runny paste. Show the children how to spread the paste over a sheet of card with a thick paintbrush. Dip the end of a matchstick into the food colouring and make small dots on the icing. Tell the children to watch as the dots spread out to become spidery, frost patterns. Say that they are like the patterns that can be seen in frost on wintry mornings. Encourage the children to describe what they notice.

Display

Make the word mobile by hanging the words from a large card hexagon on which a snowflake has been drawn with a silver or blue pen. Hang the mobile above a table on which the icing sugar frost patterns have been laid.

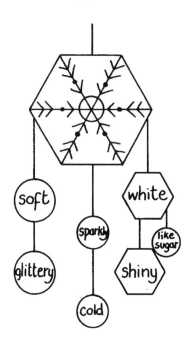

Make a snowy background on a large board. Use black paper for the sky and white for a hilly landscape. Cut around the children's self portraits. Let the children choose where their pictures to go. Invite them to cut circles from white paper to use as snowflakes falling from the sky.

Week 5
Measuring and forcasting the weather

Personal, Social and Emotional Development

- Talk about the importance of weather forecasts. Discuss outdoor activities done at weekends and holidays. Invite suggestions for the forecasts that would be desired for each of the activities. Are there any activities that can only take place on sunny days? (PS2, 3)
- Set out the role play area as a weather station. Include a telephone, globe, atlas, map and weather symbols. Encourage children to enjoy giving forecasts for imaginary, telephone queries. (PS7)

Communication, Language and Literacy

- Make a collection of pictures from around the world that show extreme weather conditions. As a group suggest words to describe the weathers. Discuss why it would be useful to have a forecast of weathers such as a tornado or heavy rain. (L3, 8)
- Provide maps of the United Kingdom on which children can enjoy writing and drawing weather forecasts. Encourage the children to sound out the words and to make phonetically plausible attempts for words such as sun, wind and fog. (L11, 18, 19)

Problem Solving, Reasoning and Numeracy

- Make a collection of weather maps cut from newspapers. Use the maps for counting practice. How many suns are there? Are there any clouds? How many clouds and suns are there altogether? Are there more suns or clouds? (N4, 8)
- Remind children of the Beaufort scale. Use the paintings the children did for number line activities. Match the pictures to their numbers. Give descriptions of numbers and ask the children to stand by them. (N3)

Knowledge and Understanding of the World

- Investigate whether 'weather sayings' are true. Possibilities to test include 'Red sky at night, shepherd's delight. Red in the morning, shepherd's warning.'; 'Rain before seven, Fine by eleven.'; and 'If March comes in like a lion, It goes out like a lamb. If it comes in like a lamb, It goes out like a lion.' (K3)
- Provide a selection of boxes (eg cereal packets), glues, tapes, papers, pens, crayons and chalks for children to choose their own materials to make a television with a weather forecast. Use the televisions for role play. (K5, 6)
- Make a collection of weather symbols. Challenge the children to make new ones (e.g. kite for wind). Use the symbols to record the weather at the end of each day. (K3)
- Make a weather wheel for each child. Encourage them to draw their own symbols for the different weathers and to use them each day for two weeks to record the weather. (K3)

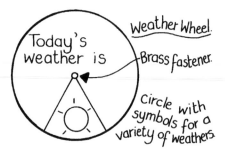

Physical Development

- Tell a story of waking, listening to a weather forecast and dressing for the weather. Encourage the children to mime to the tale and to make suggestions for the weathers and what to wear. (PD1, 2)
- Talk about signs that give a clue to the weather (e.g. wind blowing streamers and bubbles; people wearing Wellington boots to splash in puddles indicates rain and shadows show sun). Over the week, enjoy playing outside using equipment to reflect the weather. (PD7)

Creative Development

- Make windmills (see activity opposite). (CD3)
- Use white and black wax crayons/candles and watery paints to paint snowy landscapes (see activity opposite). (C5, 6)
- Enjoy singing 'Here we go round the mulberry bush, on a cold and frosty morning'. Change the words to include a range of weathers and appropriate actions for the chosen forecast. (e.g. 'This is the way we splash in the sea on a warm and sunny morning'.) (C4, 5)

Activity: Spinning Windmills

Learning opportunity: Making windmills to measure wind speed

Early Learning Goal: Creative Development. Children should explore colour, texture, shape, form and space in... three dimensions.

Resources: Windmills cut from stiff white card; felt pens; example windmill;

Key vocabulary: Wind, blow, round, sails, windmill.

Organisation: Small group

What to do: Show the children the example windmill. Demonstrate how the sails can turn and how they are made. Ask the children what they think would happen to the sails on a calm day when there was no wind. Then ask what would happen on a windy day. Explain that the harder the wind blows the faster the sails will turn. Watching the sails can tell people how hard the wind is blowing.

Give each child a windmill base on which to draw windows, a door, flowers etc. Next work with individual children to fold and glue the sails.

When complete and dry enjoy taking the windmills outside to test the wind strength.

Activity: Wax resist landscapes

Learning opportunity: Painting with watery paints over wax to make winter landscapes.

Early Learning Goal: Creative Development. Children should use their imagination in art and design... They will express and communicate their ideas, thoughts and feelings by using a widening range of materials...

Resources: Black and white wax crayons; watery blue, orange and pink paints; white A3 sized paper; pictures of winter landscapes

Key vocabulary: Wax, blue, orange, pink, white, snow, frost, winter, landscape

Organisation: Small group.

What to do: Draw a snowman with white wax crayon and a fir tree with the black. Show the children how when watery paint is painted over the paper it does not settle where the wax is.

Remind the children of the weather saying, 'Red sky at night, shepherd's delight. Red in the morning, shepherd's warning.'. Explain that they are going to paint winter landscapes to show a red night or morning sky. Ask them to draw houses, people, trees and other things they want in their scenes with white and black crayons. Then provide the watery paints for the sky.

Display

Make a hilly background with different shades of green sugar paper for displaying the windmills. Place a table in front of the display so that the children can blow the windmills at a distance without leaning on and squashing them! On the table, put out a selection of the televisions and weather wheels for the children to use to make up forecasts. Above the weather station at varying heights hang weather symbols and weather words written in large print above the weather station at varying heights.

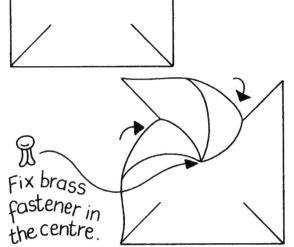

Fix brass fastener in the centre.

Week 6
Using the weather

Personal, Social and Emotional Development
- Use magazines and travel brochures to make a group patchwork of pictures that show the weather being used (see activity opposite). (PS8)
- Make a collection of items that use the weather (e.g. kite, solar powered calculator, wind chimes, washing line, toy yacht, skates, jug of water). Talk about ways that we use the weather. (PS8)

Communication, Language and Literacy
- Write a group poem that explains how the weather is used. Begin each new verse with the lines 'How do we use rain/snow/sun etc? We use … for …' (L1, 4)
- Label A3 sized pieces of paper with different weathers. Ask children to draw pictures of things they like to do in the weather written on their page. Where appropriate ask the children to write a sentence about what they are doing. Place the pictures in clear plastic wallets to make a group big book. Use freezer bag ties to fasten the pages together. (L11, 17, 19)
- Enjoy sharing storybooks that have weather as a focus (see resource list). (L4)

Problem Solving, Reasoning and Numeracy
- Enjoy counting with the snowman counting rhyme (see activity opposite). (N1, 2)
- Use a washing line with numbered articles of clothing for number recognition activities. Ask the children to peg up given numbers and to move them around the line according to instructions. (N3)
- Enjoy playing with large, solar powered calculators. Encourage the children to recognise numbers to nine. Role a die. Ask the children to enter on the calculators numbers that are the same, less than and more than the ones shown on the die. (N3, 6)

Knowledge and Understanding of the World
- Investigate whether clothes dry best on a windy or sunny day. Involve the children in washing dolls clothes and pegging them on a line on a windy day. Repeat this with the identical clothes on a sunny day. Before investigating encourage the children to predict which method will be best and to say why. (K3, 4)

- Show the group shop bought wind chimes. Help the children to realize that the longest tubes make the lowest sounds. Provide materials such as plastic and card tubes in a variety of sizes, metal spoons and pieces of wood to hang outside on a windy day. Encourage the children to notice how the wind shakes the wind chimes to make a sound. (K3, 4, 5)

Physical Development
- Enjoy using large climbing equipment and slides to pretend to go sledging in the snow. (PD3)
- Play a follow my leader type game in which the leader is the kite and the children are the tail. (PD1, 2)

Creative Development
- Enjoy singing songs and nursery rhymes that mention the weather (e.g. 'Incy wincy spider'; 'Here we go round the mulberry bush', 'Doctor Foster went to Gloucester', songs from *Harlequin 44 Songs Round the Year* chosen by David Gadsby. Invite the children to select percussion instruments to represent the weathers. (C4)
- Paint pictures to show how people use the wind, rain and sun. (C3, 5)
- Make winter landscapes inside shoeboxes. Provide a variety of materials for children to choose from. (C2, 5)

Activity: Weather Patchwork

Learning opportunity: Collaborating to make a group collage, patchwork.

Early Learning Goal: Personal and Social Development. Children should work as a part of a group or class taking turns and sharing fairly...

Resources: Travel brochures, magazines, mail order catalogues, 20cm x 20cm squares of white paper; glue sticks, scissors.

Organisation: Small group.
Key vocabulary: Names of weathers and articles cut from the magazines.

What to do: Show the children a travel brochure with photos of people skiing. Ask what the people are doing. What kind of weather is best for skiing? In what other ways do people have fun in the snow? Ask the children to look for pictures of skiing, building snowmen, sledging and snowboarding.

Show the children brochures with people in the sun. Ask them to cut out pictures of people having fun in the sun. Finally look in the mail order catalogues for other items that use the weather such as umbrellas, parasols over patio tables; rotary clothes driers etc.

Explain to the children that the things they cut out are to make collages showing how people use the weather. They will be put together to make a group patchwork. Remind children of routines for sharing resources and practical points for gluing and using scissors safely. Help them to understand why the routines are important.

Activity: Snowman counting rhyme

Learning opportunity: Enjoying counting with a number rhyme.

Early Learning Goal: Problem Solving, Reasoning and Numeracy. Children should say and use number names in order in familiar contexts. They should count reliably up to ten everyday objects.

Resources: Picture of a snowman

Key vocabulary: Numbers to ten; remain, snowman, snowmen.

Organisation: Whole group sitting on the floor.

What to do: Show the children a picture of a snowman. Talk about the joy of using snow to build snowmen. Tell the children that their fingers are snowmen standing in a line. Ask them to hold up three fingers. Recite the snowman rhyme.

Three snowmen stand in a line
(Hold up three fingers)
On a cold and frosty day,
(Rub as if cold)
The sun shines down and melts one
(Put down one finger)
As I go out to play.
Drip, drop goes the snow
(Fingers mime dripping)
As it turns to rain.
(Fingers mime dripping)
How many snowmen in the line
(Fingers stand in line)
Smile and remain?
(Count the remaining snowmen/man)

Encourage the children to join in with the actions and to work out how many snowmen remain. Over the week repeat the rhyme changing the starting number of snowmen and the number that melt.

Display
Make a wall of the shoebox scenes. Write/draw on a large sheet of paper, a list of 'I spy' things to look for within the scenes. Display the paintings of people using the weather on a large board with a sign asking people what they like to do when it is sunny weather. Change the sign each couple of days to depict different weathers. Put up the weather patchwork as a grid with black border roll to separate the patches.

Bringing It All Together

The weather day

Talk to the children about extreme weather conditions that have caused problems for people. Take care though, to do this in a sensitive way that will not provoke fear. If there has been a recent weather disaster use this as the focus for the weather day and raise money for this cause. Alternatively a developing country affected by flooding or drought might be another option. Talk about how the weather has affected the people's lives.

The weather day is best held outside of the group's normal meeting so that the children can attend with their carers and make full use of the planned activities.

Preparations

Make plans for a variety of weather focused games that the children and carers may pay small amounts of money to have a go on. These could include:

- Throwing or kicking white balls (snowballs) at a given target;
- Pinning the tail on a kite within a picture;
- Seeing how many clothes pegs can be taken off or put on a clothes line in twenty seconds;
- Blindfolded drawing of an umbrella;
- Throwing Wellington boots (a large space is needed, preferably outside, as the boots do not always travel in the intended direction!);
- Seeing how many pairs can be found in a minute from a collection of cut out boots. The boots should be in a variety of sizes, colours and patterns so that they can easily be identified as pairs;
- Finding a sweet from under an upturned seaside bucket. Set out 6 buckets and change the placing of the sweet after each go.

Ask parents for unwanted jigsaws and books that have weather as a focus. Also ask for clothes that children would enjoy buying for dressing up, to suit a range of weathers, and accessories such as garlands, fans and safe umbrellas and sunglasses. Price these items for small amounts for weather stalls.

Ask for volunteers willing to run a game or stall, provide weather themed biscuits (e.g. ones decorated with white icing or shaped like kites, umbrellas and snowmen) or look after a craft activity set up by the group. Ideas for quick activities that children enjoy are:

- Making kite shaped badges;
- Making pop out snowman cards;
- Colouring on large sunglasses frames cut from stiff card;
- Decorating sunhats for teddies made from folded squares of stiff paper;
- Decorating boots cut from black card with bright coloured and/or shiny stickers.

Costumes

Invite the children and their carers to come in costumes to show as many weathers as possible (e.g. Someone might wear Wellington boots (rain); sunglasses (sun) and a bobble hat (snow).) Have a fancy dress competition with small prizes for all who enter and umbrella and sun shaped medals for the winners.

The Weather Day

Check weather displays are complete and eye catching. Ensure there are posters that indicate clearly who will benefit from the money raised. Invite a person chosen by the children to open the weather day. Involve the children with their carers in helping to run the stalls for short intervals of time. Encourage the visitors to enjoy the activities and to look at the Weather displays. Finish by singing songs that have been learnt during the Weather project.

Resources

Resources to collect

- Old white sheets.
- Weather maps cut from newspapers.
- Mail order catalogues and travel brochures.
- Clear plastic bottles with lids.
- Pictures to show extreme weather conditions (newspaper photos of flooding, hurricanes, drought).
- Film canisters.
- Solar powered calculators.
- Things that use the weather (washing line, toy yacht).
- Digital camera.
- Small fir cones.
- White socks.
- Outline map of Great Britain to photocopy.
- Paper bowls to fit a child's head.
- CD or cassette of 'stormy music' (for example 'Spring' from *The Four Seasons* by Vivaldi).

Everyday resources

- Large and small boxes for modelling.
- Paper and card of different weights, colours and textures (for example, sugar paper, shiny paper).
- Dry powder paints for mixing and ready-mixed paints.
- Different sized paint brushes, from household brushes to thin brushes for delicate work, and a variety of paint mixing containers.
- A variety of drawing and colouring pencils, crayons, pastels, felt pens.
- Additional decorative and finishing materials such as sequins, foils, glitter, tinsel, shiny wool and threads, beads, pieces of textiles, parcel ribbon.
- Table covers.
- Dowel.
- Lentils.
- Icing sugar.
- Desiccated coconut.
- Salt.
- White modelling dough.

Stories

- *One Snowy Night* by Nick Butterworth (Collins Picture Lions).
- *After the Storm* by Nick Butterworth (Collins Picture Lions).

- *Noah's Ark* by Lucy Cousins (Walker Books).
- *Jolly Snow* by Jane Hissey (Red Fox).
- *Splash* by Jane Hissey (Red Fox).
- *The Other Goose* by Judith Kerr (Picture Lions).
- *Elmer and the Wind* by David McKee (Red Fox).
- *Elmer in the Snow* by David McKee (Red Fox).
- *Winnie at the Seaside* by Korky Paul and Valerie Thomas (Oxford University Press).
- *Winnie in Winter* by Korky Paul and Valerie Thomas (Oxford University Press).

Songs and rhymes

- *Harlequin 44 Songs Round the Year* chosen by David Gadsby (A & C Black).
- *Okki-tokki-unga Action Songs for Children* chosen by Beatrice Harrop, Linda Friend and David Gadsby (A & C Black).
- *Twinkle, Twinkle Chocolate Bar* compiled by John Foster (Oxford).
- *Alfie's Weather* by Shirley Hughes (Red Fox).
- *Out and About through the year* by Shirley Hughes (Walker Books).

Information for adults

- *The Early Years Foundation Stage: Setting the Standards for Learning, Development and Care for Children from birth to five* (Department for Children, Schools and Families).

Collecting Evidence of Children's Learning

Monitoring children's development is an important task. Keeping a record of children's achievements, interests and learning styles will help you to see progress and will draw attention to those who are having difficulties for some reason. If a child needs additional professional help, such as speech therapy, your records will provide valuable evidence.

Records should be the result of collaboration between group leaders, parents and carers. Parents should be made aware of your record keeping policies when their child joins your group. Show them the type of records you are keeping and make sure they understand that they have an opportunity to contribute. As a general rule, your records should form an open document. Any parent should have access to records relating to his or her child. Take regular opportunities to talk to parents about children's progress. If you have formal discussions regarding children about whom you have particular concerns, a dated record of the main points should be kept.

Keeping it manageable

Records should be helpful in informing group leaders, adult helpers and parents and always be for the benefit of the child. The golden rule is to make them simple, manageable and useful.

Observations will basically fall into three categories:
- **Spontaneous records:** Sometimes you will want to make a note of observations as they happen, for example, a child is heard counting cars accurately during a play activity, or is seen to play collaboratively for the first time.

- **Planned observations:** Sometimes you will plan to make observations of children's developing skills in their everyday activities. Using the learning opportunity identified for an activity will help you to make appropriate judgements about children's capabilities and to record them systematically.

To collect information:
- talk to children about their activities and listen to their responses;
- listen to children talking to each other;
- observe children's work such as early writing, drawings, paintings and 3D models. (Keeping photocopies or photographs is useful.)

Sometimes you may wish to set up 'one off' activities for the purposes of monitoring development. Some pre-school groups, for example, ask children to make a drawing of themselves at the beginning of each term to record their progressing skills in both co-ordination and observation. Do not attempt to make records after every activity!

- **Reflective observations:** It is useful to spend regular time reflecting on the children's progress. Aim to make some brief comments about each child every week.

Informing your planning

Collecting evidence about children's progress is time consuming and it is important that it is useful. When you are planning, use the information you have collected to help you to decide what learning opportunities you need to provide next for children. For example, a child who has poor pencil or brush control will benefit from more play with dough or construction toys to build the strength of hand muscles.

Example of recording chart

Name: Samuel Hardcastle		D.O.B. 1.2.04		Date of entry: 13.9.08	
Term	**Personal, Social and Emotional Development**	**Communication, Language and Literacy**	**Problem Solving, Reasoning and Numeracy**	**Knowledge and Understanding of the World**	**Physical Development**	**Creative Development**
ONE	Happy to say good-bye to mother. Enjoys collaborative play. 20.9.08 EMH	Enjoys listening to stories. Particularly enjoys rhymes. Can write first name. Often reverses 's'. Good pencil grip. 20.10.08 EMH	Is able to say numbers to ten and count accurately five objects. Recognises and names circles. 5.11.08 BM	Very eager to ask questions. Loves to carry out experiments. Enjoyed observing frost patterns. 16.10.08 LSS	Very flexible. Can balance on one leg. Loved miming dressing for rain. Does not like the feel of playdough. 16.10.08 SJS	Made a wonderful spider's web. Loves glitter and glue! Enjoys painting and particularly when mixing own colours. 16.10.08 RL
TWO						
THREE						

Skills overview of six-week plan

Week	Topic Focus	Personal, Social and Emotional Development	Communication, Language and Literacy	Problem Solving, Reasoning and Numeracy	Knowledge and Understanding of the World	Physical Development	Creative Development
1	Sunny days	Listening; Expressing emotions; Understanding what is right and wrong	Listening; Talking; Extending vocabulary; Finding rhymes	Counting; Recognising numbers; Comparing; Recognising shapes	Observing; Talking; Identifying natural features	Moving with control; Using outside toys; Being aware of body changes; Handling tools	Painting; Cutting; Constructing
2	Rain and clouds	Listening; Understanding what is right and wrong; Talking about feelings	Listening; Responding to poems; Writing	Counting; Recognising numbers; Sorting	Comparing; Describing; Investigating; Making models	Moving with control and coordination; Showing awarness of space, themselves and others; Using small equipment	Painting; Cutting; Making collage
3	Stormy days	Showing feelings; Responding to significant experiences; Working as part of a group; Taking turns	Writing labels; Listening and responding to stories	Counting; Recognising numbers; Using shapes; Comparing lengths	Investigating; Observing; Asking questions; Identifying features	Moving with control and coordination in safety; Using tools with increasing control; Using small equipment	Playing percussion instruments; Composing; Painting; Finger painting
4	Ice, frost and snow	Being aware of others' needs; Understanding what is right and wrong; Talking; Being confident to try activities	Responding to a story; Writing; Recognising sounds; Extending vocabulary	Counting; Recognising numbers; Comparing weights	Talking; Observing; Investigating; Comparing; Asking questions; Identifying features	Moving with control and imagination; Using construction materials	Using materials; Cutting; Constructing
5	Measuring and forcasting the weather	Listening; Speaking; Forming good relationsips; Maintaining attention	Listening; Discussing; Making phonetically plausible attempts to write words	Counting; Recognising numbers; Developing ideas of addition and subtraction	Comparing; Constructing; Selecting tools	Using small and large equipment; Moving with imagination, control, coordination and in safety	Constructing; Singing; Wax resist; Painting
6	Using the weather	Collaborating; Talking; Listening; Taking turns	Listening to stories; Writing; Collaborating to write a group poem	Recognising numbers; Counting; Comparing	Observing; Investigating; Comparing; Asking questions; Talking; Constructing	Moving with imagination, control, coordination and in safety	Using materials; Painting; Singing; Playing percussion instruments

Practical Pre-School Books

Home links

The theme of 'Weather' lends itself to useful links with children's homes and families. Through working together children and adults gain respect for each other and build comfortable and confident relationships.

Establishing partnerships
- Keep parents informed about the topic and the themes for each week. By understanding the work of the group, parents will enjoy the involvement of contributing ideas, time and resources.
- Photocopy the parent's page for each child to take home.
- Invite friends, childminders and families to share in the 'Weather day'.

Visiting enthusiasts
- Invite adults to come in and talk about enjoying holidays where weather has been important (for skiing, windsurfing, snowboarding, snorkeling, cycling, walking.).
- Invite adults to come in and talk about times they have experienced droughts, floods or other extreme weather conditions.

Resource requests
- Ask parents to contribute left-over wallpaper, fabric, wool, shiny materials and so on, that could be used for collages, model making and sorting activities.
- Catalogues, greetings cards and colour supplement magazines are invaluable for collage work and a wide range of interesting activities.

The 'Weather day'
- It is always useful to have extra adults at times such as the 'Weather day'. Involve them in running craft activities and stalls.
- Ask carers to donate unwanted weather themed items such as books, jigsaws, clothing and refreshments.